Ro's House

Written by Susan Reid
Illustrated by Teresa Culkin-Lawrence

Simon sat on a packing case in the kitchen. "I don't like it here. I wish we hadn't moved. I wish we still had our old house," he said.

"I miss our old house, too," said Simon's mother, "but I'm sure that we'll soon be happy here. Just wait until you make some new friends."

Simon's mother finished cutting up the vegetables.

"Why don't you take Rosie a snack?" she said. "You can ask her if she feels homesick, too."

"Rosie doesn't need to feel homesick! We brought her house with us," said Simon.

"I wish I was a guinea pig," he said, as he squeezed between two packing cases to reach the back door.

Simon bent down and lifted the lid of the hutch. "You don't know how lucky you are, Rosie," he said. "I had to leave *my* house behind."

But Rosie was gone. The wire must have been torn when the hutch was in the back of the car.

Simon looked for Rosie everywhere. But she wasn't in the garden. She wasn't in the garage. Simon even looked inside all the packing cases in the house.

Finally Simon's mother said, "You'll never find her on your own, Simon. There's Mr. Miller, our new neighbour. Perhaps he's seen Rosie."

9

Simon walked shyly over to where Mr. Miller was watering his garden.

"My guinea pig has escaped. Her name's Rosie. Have you seen her?" he asked.

"An escaped guinea pig, you say? I don't think she's here, but we'd better look in my vegetable patch. Come on!"

11

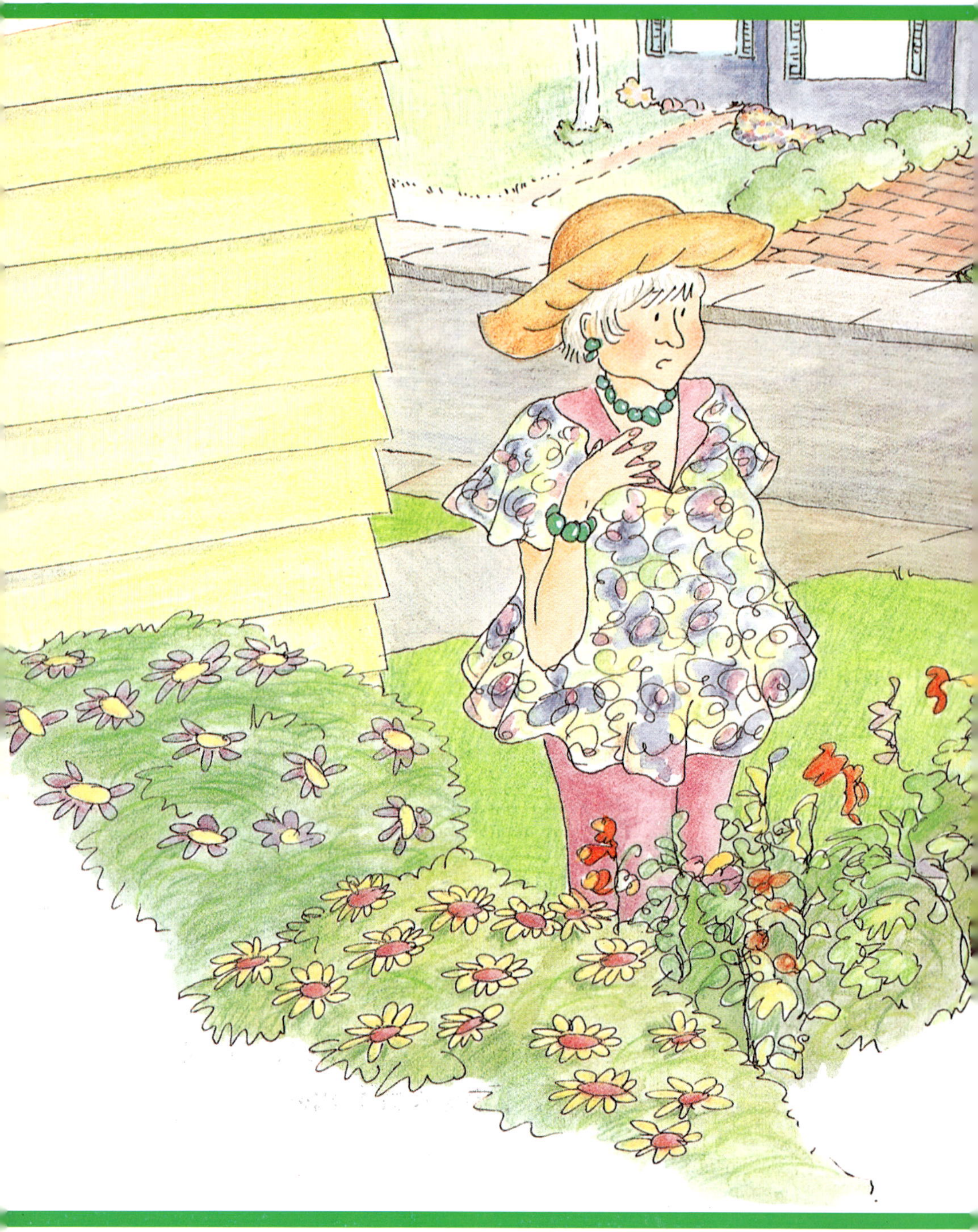

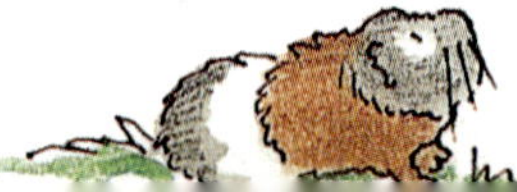

"No, Rosie's not here," said Mr. Miller. "Let's go and ask Miss Davis, your new neighbor on the other side."

"No," said Miss Davis. "I've been in my garden all day and I haven't seen a guinea pig."

"Let's ask Nick," said Miss Davis, and she called out to one of the children riding past. "Have you seen a guinea pig anywhere? Rosie has escaped."

"You've moved into number 32, haven't you?" the tallest boy asked Simon.

"Yes, do you live near here?"

"We all do," said the smallest boy. "And Nick keeps guinea pigs, too, don't you Nick?"

"Come and see them. Perhaps your guinea pig is visiting," said Nick.

But Rosie wasn't there.

"That's a great hutch!" said Simon.

"I made it," said Nick proudly. "Now, let's look for Rosie."

15

They went to almost every house in the street. Then suddenly . . .

"There she is!" yelled Nick.

"There she is!" yelled Simon.

They raced into Mrs. Field's garden, but Rosie was too fast. She darted from one plant to another. Her little nose was twitching. She was having a wonderful time.

Mrs. Field came out into the garden.
"What's going on?" she asked.
"Perhaps I can help."

Mrs. Field began to think that her garden would be trampled flat.

"FREEZE!" she yelled, and everyone stood still. "We're frightening her. Let's stand still and wait until she comes out. Then we'll grab her."

So they stood very still.

Just then Mr. Field arrived home and found his garden full of people, all standing as still as statues.
"What are you all doing?" he asked in surprise.

"Sshh, we're waiting for Rosie," whispered Mrs. Field.

The next door neighbour looked over the bushes and stared in surprise. But before she could ask what they were doing . . .

"Sshh," whispered Mrs. Field. "We're waiting for Rosie."

A delivery van pulled up next door. "Are you playing statues?" the driver laughed. "Can I play, too?"

Mrs. Field began to whisper, "Sshh, we're waiting for . . ." but just then Rosie darted out from under a bush and everyone dived to grab her.

Suddenly there was a huge pile of people all whooping and yelling.

And underneath was Simon, with Rosie safely in his arms.

Everyone wanted to see Rosie. She was quite a star.

Simon turned to Nick, "Do you think you could help me to build a hutch like yours so that Rosie doesn't escape again?"

"Sure," said Nick. "When do we start?"

"Mum, we've found Rosie!" called Simon. "Nick and I are going to build her a new hutch with this old wood and wire that Mrs. Field gave us. I really think that Rosie would like a new house, too."